SAVOR THE
LOVE

CAPTURING THE MOMENTS THAT MATTER MOST

JENNIFER L. FABIANO

WESTBOW
PRESS
A DIVISION OF THOMAS NELSON

WestBow Press books may be ordered through booksellers or by contacting:

WestBow Press
A Division of Thomas Nelson
1663 Liberty Drive
Bloomington, IN 47403
www.westbowpress.com
1-(866) 928-1240

ISBN: 978-1-4497-0162-8 (sc)

Library of Congress Control Number: 2010926339

Printed in the United States of America

WestBow Press rev. date: 7/21/2010

For Tony and Veronica.
Thank you for keeping me in the moment.

Acknowledgments

*W*riting a book is a solitary endeavor, but getting it published is a long process which requires many "cheerleaders." I'm lucky to have so many cheerleaders to thank.

To my beloved husband Brian—thank you for always believing in me, no matter what. You set the bar high, but then you help me reach it.

Thank you to all the wonderful women of Wise Women Write™. I couldn't have done this without you. Your encouragement and support pushed me forward. The sheer fact that this book finally made it into print is due, in large part, to your gentle (and sometimes not so gentle) nudges.

To our fearless leader of Wise Women Write™, Diane—thank you from the very bottom of my heart. And from the top and sides. You've been my "head cheerleader" all along. You've taught me to be a better writer, a better mother, a better person and a better friend. Your talent continues to amaze me. The friendship that we share is precious, and I am blessed to have you in my life.

To my mom—your quiet encouragement always gives me strength. Your example as a mother continues to inspire me every day. I cherish our close relationship and love you dearly.

To my treasured friend Lori—thank you for always reminding me to "write it down." Your gentle, constant reminders helped make this book a reality.

To my son Tony—thank you for your thought-provoking questions, soul-searching observations and for always being you, an old soul. You've taught me to relish every moment together.

To my daughter Veronica—thank you for helping me see the world through your beautiful, fun-loving and empathetic eyes. You've taught me the importance of being spontaneous and making time for hugs and fun.

To all the wonderful women in my life—thank you for being there as we travel on this magical journey called "motherhood" together.

Finally, and most importantly, I thank God for His love and guidance and for the blessing that is my family. His abundance is never ending.

Foreword

*A*s the founder of Wise Women Write, I am dedicated to helping women use the power of words to write about the ordinary and not-so-ordinary moments of their lives. Jennifer was in one of my groups, and I remember the spring day when she and I first met for coffee outside the group setting. The subject of book writing came up. Jennifer told me about her journals that had survived her family's house fire and her dream of turning the material into a book. I encouraged her to transfer the written journal contents to her computer as a first step and then watched her book take shape. Now, two years after that meeting, she has birthed *Savor the Love*.

Since I am such a proponent of journaling, recently a young woman told me a story that proves the value of a book like *Savor the Love*. As a teenager, she discovered a journal her parents had written about her when she was a baby. The irony is that when she came across the journal, she thought her parents hated her because of the punishment they had just imposed on her. She actually uncovered the journal when forced to spend a lot of time being grounded in her room. As soon as she began reading, her anger and frustration with her parents melted away as she realized the depths of their love. Photographs or a scrapbook just wouldn't have had the same effect. Words speak. They are powerful tools, especially when they're read many years after they're written. Can you imagine your child's heart overflowing and savoring *your* love many years from now when they read the words you write about them and realize how much you love them—both then and now?

I regret that someone didn't hand me this book when my children were small. I didn't begin writing and journaling until my four daughters were in their teens and young adulthood, and at that self-conscious age, they didn't always see the value of the stories a mother would care to tell about *them*. The teen years were fresh in my mind; childhood stories had faded into the mist of my memory. If only I had kept a journal that I could access to refresh my memory of those long-forgotten precious moments! Whenever anyone told me that kids grow up so fast, I didn't exactly believe it. But now, as I look back at my twenty-eight years of motherhood, those years spent raising four children blend into one rather blurry hunk of time. As parents, we can't wait until our baby can walk and talk. But it all goes by so fast! Now whenever I see a mother with a baby or a toddler, I tell them, "Write down the moments! You will forget and your cute little toddler will disappear into the acne and hormonal teenagers and then poof—your sweet little child will be gone and out on their own!"

Every parent needs a book like *Savor the Love.* No one witnesses our children's life like a parent. The word "journal" literally means "a day" and is taken from Old French "journee" which meant "a day's travel." When we witness and write down small moments from our children's day, we create for them a history of where they have traveled. It doesn't taken great writing skills or talent or a knack for words. It just takes a commitment to preserving the moments of childhood before they're gone forever. Jennifer has given each and every parent who picks up this book a precious opportunity to turn ordinary days into wonderful memories. All it takes is a pen and a willingness to record the moments of an ordinary day. You cannot slow down childhood, but you can capture it—with a pen, one word at a time.

Keep Writing,

Diane Owens
www.WiseWomenWrite.com

Introduction

Angry, red flames shot from our upstairs and downstairs windows. As I watched in horror from my front lawn, I never imagined that this traumatic event would inspire a book. We lost nearly everything in that fire, but three journals I had filled with memorable moments of what my children said and did as they grew up, miraculously survived—a bit sooty, but still legible.

Once we had rebuilt, moved back in and settled down again, I kept thinking about these journals and how they had been spared. I knew it had to be for a reason. Then one day, I picked up one of the journals and read a few entries to my children, then 9 and 11. They smiled or laughed out loud, but did not remember saying and doing most of what I had written. As our musings and reminiscing filled the afternoon, I was thankful that I had chosen to record these precious stories, more valued than gold. How could I influence other parents to capture those fleeting years like I had done? *Savor the Love* was born.

As a young mother of two small children, I barely had time to shower, but I still made time to write. When the kids were asleep and the house was quiet, I would make a cup of tea and open the page of a journal. I would record the remarkable things my children had said and done, sometimes laughing to myself and sometimes wiping a tear or two. I had started doing this as soon as they began talking. How many times have we, as parents, heard or seen our young children say or do something cute or poignant and we tell ourselves, "I've got to remember that." But, do we? Not only had my children forgotten some of the things I had recorded, but I had too!

Though scrapbooking is very popular these days, visual images capture only one part of the story. What about the purity and magic of a young child's mind? What about all of the questions and comments our children throw at us as they try to make sense of the world. I especially remember my son asking me, "Does God have a wife?" and my daughter's plea, "Stay here by me, Momma, for weeks and days and months" because I captured them in my journal.

Many of the stories and quotes in *Savor the Love* are spiritual in nature and mention God directly. You can feel our family's faith woven into the questions and stories. In addition, Bible verses are sprinkled throughout the book as a further reminder of our Christian faith.

It's easy for you to capture the sparkling moments of your children's childhood in this journal—just keep it handy and grab a pen. Keep it in your purse, in the car, wherever you will remember to savor the love. Be in the present with your children, and keep your eyes and ears open. Put down your cell phone and your laptop and focus on the moments right in front of you. Childhood is so precious and fleeting. These special moments will be gone quickly, and you'll wish you had taken just a moment here and there to capture them.

So, grab a pen, be in the moment and savor the love!

> *"I can do everything in my life myself except get the stuff on top of the frig and if I had a ladder I could do that, too."*
>
> **Tony, age 3-1/2**

"I like the desert better than the forest but I like the smell of fresh cut wood—it smells like baked beans—yum!"

Veronica, age 3-1/2

*Even a child is known by
his deeds, by whether what
he does is pure and right.*

Proverbs 20:11

We've been watching the Little Mermaid on the Disney Channel a lot lately. Tony asked me, "How does God make people?" I said, "It's a miracle." He said, "Does he use a magic trident like Ariel's father?"

Tony, age 3-1/2

I tucked Tony in for the night, and he said, "Good night, Momma, have sweet dreams because I love you."

Tony, age 3

Train up a child in the way he should go, and when he is old he will not depart from it.

Proverbs 22:6

Veronica eats apples in a unique way. She doesn't like the skin but she doesn't want me to peel it. So, she bites all the skin off and spits it out in a little pile so she can get to the good stuff.

Veronica, age 1-1/2

Tony's first joke: When is a farmer mean to his corn? Pulls its ears. And he doesn't wait for the punch line—he just says it all as one fast sentence.

Tony, age 3-1/2

A wise son makes a glad father, but a foolish son is a sorrow to his mother.

Proverbs 10:1

Veronica leaves off the first letter of many words—it's so cute. She says "ish" for fish and "atch" for watch and "ater" for water. Once you know the code, she's easy to understand; it's her own unique baby-pig-latin.

Veronica, age 1-1/2

The other day Tony was being sassy out in the backyard. I told him if he didn't stop beings sassy, he'd have to come in the house. He replied, "That's the way God made me, Momma....sassy!" He saw a smile on my lips even though I tried to hide it. And he said again, "God made me sassy!"

Tony, 3 yrs

Veronica was outside barefoot and her feet got dirty. She came inside and asked for a towel. After she had cleaned her feet, she looked at all the dirt on the towel and said, "Disgusting!" Amazing vocabulary for under 2!

Veronica, age 19 months

Listen, my son, to your father's instruction and do not forsake your mother's teaching.

Proverbs 1:8

For some unknown reason, Tony has decided to call blueberries "pimpie poppie boppie pumpies." But this is only when they are dried and in trail mix, otherwise, they are plain blueberries.

Tony, age 3-1/2 yrs

Tony said something was "nasty" and I told him not to use that word. Veronica heard this and then said, "Nasty poophead!" Embellishing with the addition of "poophead" (another forbidden word) was her great idea and when she said it she smiled.

Tony, age 3-1/2, Veronica, age 1-1/2

And he took the children in his arms, put his hands on them and blessed them.

Mark 10:16

Veronica is trying to understand the differences between boys and girls. This morning, I asked her, "What do boys have?" She said, "Penises." I then asked, "What do girls have?" She said, "A house!"

Veronica, age 21 months

While tucking Tony in last night he hugged me tightly and said, "Stay here by me, Momma, for weeks and days and months!"

Tony, age 3-1/2

One morning Tony came into our bedroom. He lay down next to me and asked, "Momma, why do I get so many erections?" I told him that's just the way God made boys. He said, "Maybe it's because I'm always touching my penis!"

Tony, age 3-1/2

Oreo

"A hamster?" I asked, almost sure I must have misunderstood my daughter who was sitting in the backseat.

"Yes," she said. "A hamster. I promise I'll take care of it. Tony has his own pet, his snake, so I deserve a pet of my own, too."

Of course, her arguments were logical—she had inherited the negotiation gene from her father, the master. No trying to logic her out of this one.

"Honey, hamsters are rodents and I don't like rodents," I told her.

"But, Mom, how come you like snakes?" she asked. "Snakes are reptiles and normal moms don't like reptiles."

I guess she had me there. Hmmmm...I better try another tactic. But over the next few weeks, my protestations produced nothing of substance. She was winning and she knew it.

So that's how Oreo came to join our family. She was small, black and furry with a little white stripe that ran down under her chin. When we found her at the pet store, she was older than the other "baby" hamsters. The salesgirl said she'd "been there a long time," implying that no one wanted her anymore because she wasn't a baby. This softened both our hearts and we asked to see her.

Unlike many hamsters, when the salesgirl opened the door to her cage, Oreo came right to her and almost seemed to greet her. She didn't run and she certainly didn't bite like so many had that we had seen. This was a good sign. The salesgirl placed her in my daughter's hands and it was love at first cuddle. Thus began our journey of learning to care for, appreciate and love a hamster.

She really was adorable. The way she'd stuff food into her pouches to save for later. Or the cute way she washed her face with her tiny human-like front paws. I marveled that a small rodent could have such a large, loving personality.

Oreo helped my daughter become more independent. She didn't mind staying home alone for 20 or 30 minutes while I ran an errand because Oreo was there. She loved to hear Oreo run on her wheel in the evenings. It made her feel "not alone."

Oreo also gave my daughter a sense of accomplishment. Yes, she could care for a living creature. Yes, she could be the sole provider of food and water to this little warm-blooded pet. My daughter's confidence grew.

Hamsters, like all small mammals, have short life spans. I gently kept reminding my daughter of this.

"I know, Mom" she'd say. "But, let's just love her a lot while she's with us."

Wise words we should all take to heart with those we love.

I'm still not sure that what I felt for Oreo was love, but I do know that when I found her curled in her cage not breathing one morning, I got tears in my eyes. For Oreo and her short life. For my daughter, whose heart would break. For lost innocence.

We buried her in a pretty box in our backyard under a tree.

Drying her tears, my daughter said, "Oreo – she didn't have a long life but she was loved a lot." Well said.

Veronica still mixes up her pronouns. The other day Brian told her she was being sassy and she said, "Don't call my sassy!"

Veronica, age 23 months

Veronica is also becoming very possessive. Everything is "That's mine!" If you try to cuddle her when she doesn't want it, she says, "Leave my alone!" Unique pronoun use and possessiveness.

Veronica, age 23 months

We're at the store and Tony wants me to buy him a water pistol. So, we're at the checkout and he's begging me. Finally, I say, "Tony, we don't buy guns in this family!" He replies, "Mom, it's not a gun, it's a weapon!" Everyone in line around us starting laughing—it was cute. But I still didn't buy him the gun.

Tony, age almost 4 yrs

The father of a righteous man has great joy; he who has a wise son delights in him.

Proverbs 23:24

When we sit down to dinner and prepare to say prayers, Veronica has started saying, "My turn!" Then, she coyly says, "God is great, God is good, thank Him for food, amen!" Then, she claps and smiles as if she just gave a great performance.

Veronica, age 23 months

Tony is obsessed with Superman. He has even developed a special Superman kiss. He says, "Superman is on the way." Then, he kisses you. He also says that the third rung of his bunk bed ladder is the hug step and rung four is the kiss step. Such a cuddle-bug!

Tony, age 4

Tony has Superman pajamas that he loves to wear. When he has them on, we call him Superman. One morning we told Veronica she was Supergirl. She responded, "I not Supergirl, I Superprincess!"

**Tony, age 4,
Veronica, age 2**

If Tony hurts himself, my husband usually says, "Are you okay, bud?" Well, the other day Tony fell down and Veronica ran over to him, put her hand on his shoulder and said, "Are you okay, bud?"

**Tony age 4,
Veronica age 2**

Veronica still loves to say "no" and it sometimes makes Tony mad. We were at the store and I explained to him that toddlers (like Veronica) do that sometimes—say "no." A short while later Veronica stuck her tongue out at him. He told me about it and before I could scold her, he said, "Toddlers do that—stick out their tongues." Good logic!

**Tony age 4,
Veronica age 2**

Veronica is wanting to do everything herself. If she can't do something, we tell her, "When you're bigger, you can do, x, y and z." So now she says, "Be bigger, drive car?" Or "Be bigger, go to meetings?" Then, she added, "Be bigger Daddy buy me pink car?" I told her, "Yes, just be sure to remind Daddy of that in 14 years!"

Veronica, age 2

My father, Papa, is very sick. Last night I was crying and Tony asked me why. I told him it was because Papa is old and sick and will go to Heaven soon. Tony then said, "Momma, you'll see him again someday. When YOU get very, very, very, very old and go to heaven, you'll see him there." He's so sweet. Then he added, "I'm going to miss Papa, too."

Tony, age 4

Veronica confuses "shoulder" with "elbow." I sometimes wear my long hair in a braid over my right shoulder a lot. The other day she came to me and asked if she could have a "braid on my elbow like you" and pointed to her shoulder. It was so cute!

Veronica, age 2

After tucking Tony in he said, "Mom, I love you so much I think I'll keep you forever." Such a sweet soul.

Tony, age 4

Children, obey your parents in everything, for this pleases the Lord.

Colossians 3:20

Tony loves sharks and snakes. We've rented lots of videos on them, especially featuring the great white shark. The other night before bed, he hugged me and said, "Mom, you're a better momma than a shark." I said, "Why?" He said, "Because after they have their babies, they leave them all alone and you're going to be with me the rest of my life."

Tony, age 4-1/4

Veronica and Tony have a pretend cash register that says, "Thank you, come again" when you finish a sale. The other day I asked Veronica to close her eye so I could get the sleep dust out of it. She did and then when I was through, she smiled and said, "Thank you, come again." It was adorable. Tony has started saying it now, too. They think it's all one phrase. Thank—you—come—again.

**Tony, age 4-1/4,
Veronica, age 2-1/4**

Veronica loves to swim, as does Tony. They're both fish. He does dives and underwater tricks already. When Veronica wants to swim from one adult's arms to another's, she calls it "back and forest," instead of back and forth. They are both so awesome. God has truly blessed us.

**Tony, age 4-1/4,
Veronica, age 2-1/2**

On the way home from Disneyland in the airplane, Tony looked out the window and was in awe that we were above the clouds. He looked at me and said, "Momma, I think we're in Heaven!"

Tony, age 4-1/2

Veronica has been listening to Tony tell jokes. This is her version of a joke she told me yesterday:
Q: Why did Snow White cross the road?
A: To get to her prince!

Veronica, age 2-1/2

"Momma, I love you more than anything you buy for me or anything you cook for me!"

Tony, age 4-1/2

Our kids have such great vocabularies. When Veronica woke up the other morning she said she was cold. "I am shivering!" she said. Yesterday when deciding what to do, I said, "Let's have a party!" Tony replied, "No, let's have a celebration!" Awesome!

Tony, age 4-1/2, Veronica, age 2-1/2

Tony asked me yesterday, "Momma, can I marry Veronica?" I told him no, it's not allowed. He said, "But I love her best of all." I said he'd find a special girl to love. He said, "No, but I only like Veronica's or yours or Daddy's spit—no one else's." I changed the subject.

Tony, age 4-1/2

Veronica didn't hug her Daddy good morning so I said, "Please go give Daddy a hug." She looked at me and said, "I'll give him a hug on Thursday."

Veronica, age 2-1/2

Behold, children are a heritage from the Lord, the fruit of the womb is a reward.

Psalm 127:3

Brian and Veronica went to visit Grammy. Veronica was tired and a little whiney so Brian said that he'd "get her whatever she wanted—anything—just tell me." Veronica moaned, "No, whatever you get me, I want something different!"

Veronica, age 2-3/4

In conversation the other day I was reminding Tony that Gramma is retired. He asks how does she get money to live. I told him that you save while you work so that you can retire when you are older. He said, "You know my big bank in my room? The one with all the coins in it?" I said yes. He said, "Well, I think I'll use that for retirement." I told him that he didn't need to start saving at 4 years old but he said, "But I really want to!"

Tony, age 4-1/2

Every time we drive by the farm on Bell Road, the kids yell out, "Thanks for the ice cream!" to the cows. So cute.

Tony, age 4-1/2, Veronica, age 2-1/2

Veronica's recent grace said before dinner: "Thank you for Momma. Thank you for Daddy. Thank you for Tony and Veronica. And I never want to get old. Amen. And thank you."

Veronica, age 3

Today Veronica said, "I wish Papa would come back from Heaven." I explained that once you go to Heaven, you can't come back. Then Tony said, "Veronica, don't you remember—we were in Heaven once—before God put us in Momma's tummy." I said that's right. Tony said, "So we got back here." What deep thoughts!

**Tony, age 5,
Veronica, age 3**

Veronica asked Tony, "Where were we before we were here?" Tony answered her, "God was making us!"

**Tony, age 5,
Veronica, age 3**

*Tony tried pudding for the
first time and absolutely
loved it. He said, "This is
the best day of my life—this
and the day I was born."*

Tony, age 5-1/2

Therefore, whoever humbles himself like this child is the greatest in the Kingdom of Heaven.

Matthew 18:4

Tony was going potty and asked me through the closed door how to spell a word. I cracked the door open to tell him the answer and saw he was sitting on the toilet reading Money magazine—crazy!

Tony, age 5-1/2

Tony was invited to his "girlfriend's" birthday party—a girl from school named Alistaire. I asked him what she liked so we could get her a present: Barbies, puzzles, etc. He said, "She told me what she wanted." I said Oh? "Yes," he said, "She whispered in my ear that for her birthday she wanted me!"

Tony, age 5-1/2

Veronica can't stop making snow angels. Every time I look out the window of our cabin, she's on her back making another one. And then there's Tony, with his tongue stuck out, trying to catch the best snowflake. He then runs up to me on the porch and I ask him what he needs. He says, "I came back for another kiss from you, Mom, I'll always take more!"

**Tony, age 5-3/4,
Veronica, age 3-3/4**

We were having lunch and Veronica kept telling her Daddy not to steal her french fries but to ask first. Then, he asked her if he could have a kiss. She said, "Love is not for asking, you just give it!"

Veronica, age 4

We were in the pool and discussing fairy godmothers and angels. I said, "Some people believe in angels." Tony said, "I do because I believe in Papa."

Tony, age 6

I overheard Veronica talking to herself in her room: "Daddy's my favorite man. Momma's my favorite woman. Tony's my favorite boy and I'm my favorite self!"

Veronica, age 4

Veronica loves to run and Tony calls her his little roadrunner. The other day we were hiking and discussing our state bird, the roadrunner. Tony said, "Veronica should be our state bird because she's such a roadrunner!"

Tony, age 6

I was having Veronica pick up after herself and she got mad and said, "Momma, you're so mean!" Later that night when I was tucking her in, she said, "Momma, I hope you know that no matter what I say to you, I still love you!"

Veronica, age 3-1/2

I went with Tony's class to the zoo. At lunch, he said, "Look, my best friend is sitting next to me, my Mom's across from me and my teacher's right here, too—what a perfect day!"

Tony, age 6-1/2

My Son

My son. Fifteen years ago, when I was newly pregnant, those two words filled me with panic. How would I, the middle sister of three girls, raise a son? I didn't know anything about boys, *baby* boys, what was I going to do? After my ultrasound revealed my baby's maleness, I nervously telephoned my older sister, who was raising a son and a daughter, for moral support.

"They're so easy," she said. "Much easier than girls!" What? What did she mean, they're easier? "There's just a special mother-son bond that is so wonderful. It's hard to describe in words. You'll see."

Hmmmm. Okay. If she can do it, I can do this, I thought. I then embraced the impending birth of my son, my first child, with renewed excitement.

Shopping for baby boy clothes became a hobby – I never realized that boys, too, had 'outfits.' I purchased numerous books on raising boys and devoured them hungrily. I decorated his nursery with strong, primary colors and prepared for the arrival of this male child with eagerness and enthusiasm.

Now, looking back over the past fourteen-plus years, I finally 'get it'—this unique mother-son bond. Perhaps it was the way he wouldn't nap soundly unless he was lying on my chest all warm and slightly sweaty, able to hear my heart beat. Or, the way he had four different kinds of kisses he just had to give me each night before I tucked him in: butterfly kiss, elephant kiss, upside-down kiss and regular kiss. Or, even the way he clung to my legs, crying as if his heart was breaking, when I brought him to preschool the first two weeks.

My son. I love every version of him. The one-year-old diapered toddler with eyes full of wonder. The five-year-old basketball novice who can barely dribble. The ten-year-old beginner chef who bakes me a cake for my birthday and pancakes for Mother's Day. And, now, the fourteen-year-old man-child with a deep voice who comes up behind me and surprises me with a hug from his 6'2" bulk.

My son. Those two words seem almost implausible when I gaze down at my now sleeping teenager. He's a contradiction if there ever was one. An old soul who still has much to learn. A young boy in a man's body. A sweet, gentle spirit with a fierce competitive streak.

My son. Now, those two words can barely contain my heart.

Veronica said, "I don't like Burger King french fries or hamburgers. And I don't like their name—why can't they call it Burger Queen?"

Veronica, age 4-1/2

Tony told me that when he is scared at night from the red numbers on his digital clock he pretends to himself the numbers are yellow. "Yellow," he says, "stands for Honey Momma!" He has started calling me that all the time now—so cute!

Tony, age 6-1/2

We were at our cabin and the kids were outside playing in the snow. I couldn't see them from the window so I stepped out on the front porch and called out to tell them to stay closer to the cabin so I could watch over them. Veronica called out, "It's okay, Mom, God's watching over us!"

Veronica, age 4-1/2

The other night Tony was asking lots of questions on a variety of topics. Finally, he just smiled and said, "Momma, why do kids ask so many questions?"

Tony, age 6-1/2

*In the early morning
Tony likes to crawl into
bed between Brian and
I and cuddle—that is, if
Veronica hasn't beat him
to it! He wakes me up so
gently by kissing my cheek
softly and the first thing I
see when I open my eyes is
his angelic, smiling face!
God has given us two
angels to love and protect!
We are so blessed!*

**Tony age, 6-1/2,
Veronica, age 4-1/2**

*Veronica heard the
phrase, "Yes, ma'am"
on some television show
and now when you ask
her to do something, she
says, "Yes, ma'am." It
has become her favorite
phrase. So, we have taken
to calling her Mammy
and she likes it.*

Veronica, age 4-1/2

If a man curses his father or mother, his lamp will be snuffed out in pitch darkness.

Proverbs 20:20

Tony asked, "Does God have a wife?" I said no.

Tony, age 6-1/2

Veronica asked, "Who made God?" I explained that He always existed and always will.

Veronica, age 4-1/2

Tony loves to go to the bathroom after a big meal. The other day, at a restaurant, we waited for him while he used the restroom. He got to the car and said, "I feel great!" I asked if he always loved to go to the restroom after a meal. He said, "Yes, that's the way my world goes!"

Tony, age 6-3/4

Last night Veronica said she missed Papa. I told her I did, too, but that I would see him in Heaven when I got very old. She started crying and when I asked what's wrong she said, "I'm going to be the last one in our family to go to Heaven because I'm the youngest!" I told her that's okay. But then she said, "I want to go when you go, Momma!" I just smiled and hugged her, not able to explain that her love of life would change her mind when she got older.

Veronica, age 4-3/4

Transference

The secret to beauty has finally been revealed to me. I'm not going to package it and make millions of dollars off of it, but I am learning it firsthand.

It doesn't come in a fancy glass bottle, or a shiny blue jar, or as a series of injections you endure every three months. It's not a cream or a pill or a new work-out program. In fact, you can't buy it or borrow it. Let me explain.

My pubescent daughter is blossoming, budding and burgeoning with beauty. Her vitality and vibrancy is very evident and her chocolate-brown eyes sparkle with life untested. Her skin glows with good health and her coltish body performs at peak capacity. But, each day I feel as if my own vitality is waning; my beauty faltering and fading. Could this transference be the result of close bedfellows?

Each night, sometime between midnight and three o'clock in the morning, my daughter tiptoes into my room and gently touches my arm. I awake, lift the covers and scoot over to make room. She snuggles in close to me and quickly drifts off to sleep. I lay awake and revel in the warmth of her body, knowing deep in my soul that these days are numbered, but loving them nonetheless.

Now, thinking more about these frequent nocturnal visits which my daughter assures me are the result of a "bad dream," I think I know their true purpose: to pass on the life force from me to her. Transferring the maturity, knowledge and femininity she needs to grow up. Not only comfort does she seek, but assurance that in growing into adulthood, I will still be there—to cuddle, to slay the night demons, to soothe her slumber.

In the morning, the nighttime ritual is easily forgotten by my daughter as she faces the day with eager exuberance and energy. But for me, its memory lingers in the smell of her on my pillow and the feel of her heartbeat next to mine.

If this is what I must endure to see her growing beauty, then so be it. I will willingly go to sleep and know that each night, a small part of me will be transferred to her. And, when I look in my own mirror, I won't be saddened, knowing instead that what is fading in me, is becoming splendor in her.

(Published in *Raising Arizona Kids* Magazine, 2009.)

Veronica is writing lots of poetry lately: Red is a rose. Pink is like a pig. Purple is like grapes. Blue is like a blue doll.

Veronica, age 4-3/4

Tony was cuddling me one night and saying how much he loved me. Then, he said, "I can't describe it in words how much I love you, Momma." I told him that I didn't think we were supposed to be able to describe it in words because God created love. Tony replied, "He's a genius!" I agreed.

Tony, age 6-3/4

Tucking Veronica in one night, I said, "Thank you for being my daughter." She responded, "You should tell God thank you, not me, because He made me!"

Veronica, age 4-3/4

A wise son brings joy to his father, but a foolish son grief to his mother.

Proverbs 10:1

For Father's Day we got Brian a sound soother that plays ocean sounds, forest sounds, etc. The kids borrowed it and used it to fall asleep. Then, one night when I was tucking Veronica in, I asked her what sound she wanted to listen to. She said, "Just leave my door open. I don't need a sound soother—you guys are my sound soother." She went on to explain that she likes to fall asleep listening to us talk downstairs. What a sweetie!

Veronica, age 5

Tony said to me the other day, "Mom, I like being around you because you only get mad six times a year."

Tony, age 7

Each night when I tuck
Veronica and Tony in we
talk about where we can meet
in our dreams. Sometimes
we say we'll shrink down and
meet in the Barbie Dream
House. Other times we meet
in the snow or at the park.
But tonight she said, "Let's
meet at the airport and take
a plane to Mexico!" I have
no idea where she got that
idea but it sounds fun!

Veronica, age 5-1/2

Last night after tucking
Tony in, I still heard him
awake. So, I snuck into
his room and jumped
out and yelled, "Boo!"
He jumped. And then
he started laughing and
said, "You scared me
so bad you made my
penis wiggle!" We both
laughed and laughed!

Tony, age 7-1/2

Veronica's poem: Pink is like a pink sweet girl. Purple is like a sweet boy.

Veronica, age 5

Jesus said, "Let the little children come to me, and do not hinder them, for the kingdom of heaven belongs to such as these."

Matthew 19:14

Last night at religious education we had to write get well cards to someone we knew who was sick. No one in our family is sick so Sam, our teacher, told us about a woman at church who had cancer and said she would love some cards. Veronica wrote: I hope God sends you angels, Angels are praying for you. God is praying for you. Veronica is praying for you. Love, Veronica; Tony wrote: I hope God sends angels to protect you. Love, Tony. I think I am the one who has two angels!

**Veronica, age 5-1/2,
Tony, age 7-1/2**

Veronica and I were coming back from gymnastics one evening and I commented on how pretty the sunset looked. I said, "God paints us a beautiful sunset every night!" She said, "I don't think he uses paint, Mom, I think he uses Blowpens!" Cute!

Veronica, age 5-3/4

French Pedicure

I lay out all the supplies in front of me and squint my 47-year-old eyes at the tiny instruction sheet. Is this really written in English, I ask myself? You are very excited as you place your clean, dainty feet in front of me on the soft towel I have laid out for you. I am pleased and also nervous by the excitement in your voice. Why did I ever think I could give you a French pedicure? It must have been a fleeting moment of I'm-a-mom-so-I-can-do-anything. Those moments can be dangerous.

As I stick the little white guides on the tips of your toes, you bubble over with stories from your day. Who said what. Whose feelings got hurt. How much your Spanish teacher bugs you. Which boy is the only cute one in school. Your enthusiasm for life is infectious. And your kind, empathetic heart shines brightly through as you chatter about your many friends.

Friends. My friends sustain me, too, even in the midst of my happy 20-year marriage. But, my friends who have never had children still don't really "get me." They don't get why I have become a champion for my children's best interests. They don't get the vast amount of time I want to spend with my children. They cannot comprehend the depth of my love for my children and the fact that my heart now lives outside my body, divided in two inside these two astonishing, unpredictable humans. They also don't get how my children have made me more than I used to be – confident that I can do anything, even French pedicures without a cosmetology license.

Once I am finished embellishing your tiny toes, you are ecstatic.

"Do my fingers, too!" you exclaim. "Please?"

I'm happy that you're happy and when I look down at your toes, I smile.

"See, Mom, it looks like I went to a salon," you say. "You could be a professional!"

Your beautiful caramel chocolate eyes beseech me to attempt your fingers. I cannot refuse. I savor this closeness while you're still young enough to be impressed with me and my abilities.

I take your small, left hand in mine, savoring the warm, skin-to-skin contact, and begin again.

Tony was allowed to stay up late last night and watch a show on sharks. I asked him if it would give him bad dreams. He said no. He then added, "If I ever have bad or scary thoughts while I'm falling asleep, I just think of camels walking in a circle!" "Why?" I asked. "Because they are so silly!" He is so awesome!

Tony, age 7-1/2

An hour after tucking Veronica in, she woke up sobbing and saying, "Something's not right in the world." She couldn't be consoled so I asked her if she wanted to sleep on Tony's top bunk. She agreed. After tucking them both in, I lingered by the door and heard Tony say, "What's not right, Veronica?" She said, "I don't know." He said, "Just tell me and I'll fix it." So sweet.

**Veronica, age 6,
Tony, age 8**

The righteous man leads a blameless life; blessed are his children after him.

Proverbs 20:7

Veronica told me yesterday, "Mom, I know what God looks like: he has blue jeans and a yellow shirt and brown hair and blue eyes. And no beard or mustache." Wow. She is amazing.

Veronica, age 6

We were driving to the cabin and playing "I'm thinking of something." Veronica said, "I'm thinking of something cuddly." Tony guessed all her cuddly things and all of his cuddly things. Veronica said no. She then added, "It's almost always with you." Tony guessed more but could not guess what it was. Then, it dawned on me and I said, "It's me—Momma!" Veronica grinned and said yes!

**Veronica, age 6,
Tony, age 8**

We rented an RV and took a trip to Colorado to pick up our new puppy, Joy. We stopped at a couple KOAs and when we pulled in to the first one, Tony asked, "What does KOA stand for?" Before I could tell him, he said, "I know, Kitty On Airplane!" We all cracked up! The rest of the trip we called them Kitty On Airplanes!

Tony, age 8

The kids got their report cards yesterday and they both did awesome. When Brian was giving Veronica a goodnight kiss, he said how proud he was of her. She replied, "Tony's not the only one in this family who's getting a scholarship, you know!"

Veronica, age 6

Children, obey your parents in the Lord, for this is right.

Ephesians 6:1

I was napping at the cabin one afternoon and Veronica came into our room. She hugged me and said, "Mom, I love you more than you believe I do." With that, she left my room, me smiling.

Veronica, age 6

Tony and I were all dressed up to go on a date together. He asked Brian to take a picture of us. When Brian was done, Tony said, "I wish pictures had smell because we both smell so good tonight!"

Tony, age 8

On the way to the cabin, Veronica said, "God is the father of everything! The earth, the sky, even Texas and Alabama!"

Veronica, age 6-1/2

All your children shall be taught by the Lord, and great shall be the peace of your children.

Isaiah 54:13

When we first got Joy, we'd tether her downstairs to a kitchen chair when we needed to go upstairs. One time, Veronica came upstairs and I asked her, "Where's Joy?" She answered, "I strangled her." I said, "You mean you tethered her?" "Oh, yes," she said. She always mixed up tether and strangle. Cute.

Veronica, age 6

This is why Tony says
he plays basketball:

1. I have good friends on my team.
2. Dads pays me for scoring.
3. It's fun.
4. Dad wants me to.

Tony, age 8-1/2

Savor the Fun

"If it's not fun, why do it?" This bumper sticker from Ben & Jerry's is posted on the white magnet board in our laundry room at home, yet finding time for fun is challenging. As life gets busier, it seems to get more "serious." Fun falls to the bottom of the "To Do" list, if it ever belonged on a list at all.

Time for fun can be easy to find if you're the type of person who can throw caution to the wind, forget your responsibilities and just kick back. But, I'm not that kind of person. I feel the weight of my life's responsibilities like a heavy, wooden yoke across my shoulders, getting heavier and heavier with the added weight of my husband's, my son's and my daughter's responsibilities. I think if I truly kept one master calendar of all that we had to do, I wouldn't even get out of bed in the morning after looking at it – it's too daunting and it must weigh ten tons. Thankfully, I don't do that. I keep each list separate. I try to take each list every day in small bites, savoring the ones I can and looking at the lists like a menu to be sampled.

I should eat dessert first! Add fun to the list. I should pick fun from the menu of life and really savor it. It was so simple to do when my children were small – learning was fun, just being young was fun, each new experience, simply because it was new, was fun.

Now that my children are teenagers, the mere definition of fun is hard to pin down. Is texting your friends for hours on end fun? Is swimming with your girlfriends on a sunny Saturday fun? Is playing basketball with your buddies after school fun? Does fun *ever* include your parents when you're a teenager? That's it! Fun is being had without me – that's why it seems to have disappeared from my life.

Fun has changed and morphed into a subtle flavor, not as strong or recognizable but delicious still the same. It is the simple laugh at a radio disc jockey's joke my son and I share in the car on the way to school. Or the impromptu trip to the mall with my daughter. Or the laugh my husband and I enjoy while watching a comedy on a rare weekday evening. Tiny bites, like an appetizer menu, no more grand courses. No full meals of fun. But always remember that wise saying: Life's short, eat dessert first!

Taking Joy for a walk at the cabin one afternoon, Veronica grabbed some weeds which came off in her hands like wheat and sprinkled them on Joy's back and said, "Joy, this is what life is made of."

Veronica, age 6-1/2

We were buying toys to donate to Veronica's class at school. She was in the car with me and started singing, "Five jump ropes, two skip-its and a partridge in a pear tree!" I smiled and she smiled. She's very witty.

Veronica, age 6-1/2

When tucking Tony in last
night, he said, "Mom,
I can't wait to grow up
and be an adult!" I asked
why. He said, "Because
I'll get to vote, drive a car
and drink champagne!"

Tony, age 9

Veronica has a small white lamb with a jingle bell inside her named Lamby. She would not let me wash her for years because, as she said, "She wanted to save the smell of her babyhood." She finally did let me hand wash her the other day and now she's glad she did.

Veronica, age 7

Don't let anyone look down on you because you are young, but set an example for the believers in speech, in life, in love, in faith and in purity.

Timothy I 4:12

Veronica said, "If I had three wishes, I'd wish for 1) not to have celiac disease, 2) 1,000 more wishes, and 3) for everyone in the world to be nice."

Veronica, age 7

Wake-Up

I quickly glance at the digital kitchen clock and realize it's time to wake you. I enter the dark cave of your room and turn on a soft light. I sit down on the side of your bed and place my hand gently on your back, rubbing softly. I bend down and kiss the side of your face, relishing the comfy, warm smell of you.

"Time to get up, Sweetie," I say as I continue rubbing your strong, muscled back.

You mumble and burrow down into your covers, your feet almost off the end of the bed. At 6'2" but only 14, you're my gentle giant.

"Two more minutes," I say as I go back to the kitchen to finish my morning routine.

Standing at the granite counter, making your lunch, I think about how lucky I am to have a son like you. Smart and funny, yet serious and kind. You've always opened doors for others, loved small children and treated animals with kindness. Your size scares some people but once they realize your heart is oversized as well, they're glad to be your friend.

I must go back to your bedroom soon to wake you again and ensure that this time you do get up and shower because your days are filled from dawn to dark. Basketball and personal training (and school!) take up most of it. Your dedication at such a young age is astonishing. But your sense of fun is there, too, and you include me.

You've encouraged me to do things I never thought I'd do. We got scuba certified together and then took dives in Hawaii and the Virgin Islands. We learned to snowmobile together and enjoyed the terrain in Telluride. But we also enjoy the intellectual—watching a good movie that really makes you think. Going to see a play or other live performance and talking about it afterwards.

My love for you makes me stronger. If I can help mold such a strong, old soul, it completes me.

I walk back to your room and again open your door slowly for a final wake-up. Your bed is empty. You have begun the day.

*Your eyes saw my
unformed substance;
in your book were written,
every one of them,
the days that were
formed for me,
when as yet there was
none of them.*

Psalm 139:16

Britney Spears is playing on the car radio. Veronica says, "I hear she lip syncs. Who would they get to lip sync? Why would someone do that?" Before I could answer, she says, "See, there's still so much in this world that I don't understand yet."

Veronica, age 12

*After Tony's tonsillectomy,
we were in recovery and he
was loopy from the medication.
He said, "Momma?" And
the nurse turned and smiled
at me to hear such a term of
endearment from a 6'2" big
boy. He wanted to know what
direction he was facing. We
found out and told him. He
said he felt better knowing his
head was facing north. Later,
he said, "I want to tell you
a joke, Momma." I asked
why. "Because I need to," he
said. "Did you know Helen
Keller had a dog?" No, I said.
"Neither did she." He laughed
loudly, the medicine making
him even loopier and I laughed
watching his smiling face.*

Tony, age 14

*Children, obey your
parents in all things,
for this is well and
pleasing to the Lord.*

Colossians 3:20

The Welcome

"Mom, don't ever leave us again!"
I had been gone four days. My 13-year-old daughter hugs me fiercely and I smile, glad to have been missed.

"Seriously, Mom, we're even out of water!" she exclaims in horror.

"Water, huh? What about the kitchen faucet?" I ask, wondering to myself what the past four days had been like here at home as I pull my luggage into the laundry room. My daughter's complaint hit on the very basic of necessities. Her underlying meaning is clear: things fell apart without me and a basic human need—water (in the small bottles I kept stocked in the garage refrigerator)—had been ignored.

Although my absence from our home had been brief, it appeared to have had a large impact on my family. I almost felt guilty for being gone—almost, but not quite. I had been in Wisconsin with my mother visiting my 93-year-old grandmother who recently had a stroke. We travel well together and always get along. We reconnected with many family members and spent precious time with my grandmother. An added benefit for me was four days away from my "job." No meals to shop for, plan or cook. No lunches to make. No ferrying kids to and from school and activities. No homework to cajole my kids into doing. No wash to do. No one's needs to worry about but my own.

Don't misunderstand, I love being a wife and mother. I'm very good at my job and take it seriously. But I also feel unappreciated sometimes. I hadn't realized how a small trip away could help my family see what it is that I do. Absence really did seem to make my family grow fonder!

"I'm so glad you're home," my 15-year-old son says when we're alone. "I had to be Mr. Mom and keep the kitchen clean, load the dishwasher and keep Dad and Veronica organized. And they kept arguing—it was terrible!"

"I'm glad to be home, too," I say as I give him a big hug. In addition to chef, chauffeur, maid and housekeeper, I'm also the family peacemaker and buffer. My calm personality tempers my husband's passionate Italian nature. My daughter is just like him, and they often need a middle man (or woman) to keep them calm together. Especially during these emotionally-charged, hormone-filled teen years.

"We really missed you, Honey," my husband says as he hugs me. He then went to lie down on the comfy family room couch. "I'm exhausted—it's hard when you're gone—you do so much. So glad you're home." And with that he is soon asleep in his favorite spot, TV remote in hand.

"Dad was so mean, too!" my daughter whispers as she hugs me again and pulls me into my bedroom to cuddle. I'm enjoying this physical affection since recently she has been pushing me away, doing what all teens do when they need to gain independence in the world.

"He kept telling me to do things and then getting mad if I didn't do them right away," she cries, as if this expectation was completely unreasonable. I knew I'd hear the other side of this story from my husband later, so I enjoy the cuddles and listen while she pours out her heart.

"Just please don't ever leave again!"

I reveled in the feeling of being missed. I changed into my pajamas as my daughter recounts further episodes of parental cruelty that had occurred in my absence.

Being missed is a gift; one which moms need now and then. It's like the story of the craftsman building the cathedral—his effort and hard work is invisible. Only upon its completion, can the full impact of all the work that went into building the immense structure be truly understood. Only when my children are grown, happy and content with families of their own will I feel accomplished. But it's nice to know that the little things along the way get noticed.

Do my kids still think those water bottles just magically appear in the extra fridge, waiting for a thirsty teen to grab after school? No. And they also figured out how it is they always have clean clothes and a full pantry.

I know I need to help my kids become more independent as they get older, but for now, I can still spoil them, nurture them and be the best mom I can be. Maybe another trip in the next few months will teach even more lessons? I can't wait!

(Originally published in *Raising Arizona Kids* Magazine, 2010)

"Mom, you're different, you're the only mom who doesn't mind driving everywhere, picking us up, and stuff." I savored these words of Veronica's like a precious, unbroken sand dollar found amidst the roaring surf. I like this kind of different!

Veronica, age 13

Tony was out with friends
and so I texted him: Have
fun being 15 but be wise.
He texted me back:
Have fun being 48 but
be spontaneous.
What a wise soul!

Tony, age 15

A Full Plate

He needs to be fed.
Not the dog.
My teenage son.
A bottomless receptacle
Waiting for nourishment.
His body needs food,
Protein, carbs, fats,
Meat, potatoes, veggies,
Ice cream, donuts, cookies.
He also needs to be fed love,
Adoration, guidance, acceptance,
Wisdom, patience, knowledge,
Spooned and heaped upon his plate.
So when he's an adult
His plate is full.

Stopping by a bakery/sandwich shop to pick up lunch, I also asked for two snickerdoodles, my and Tony's favorite. I paid, she handed me the bag, and I hurried on my way. Later that afternoon, when Tony looked in the bag, there were three cookies, not two. We were both surprised. He said, "That's for all your good karma, Mom." I smiled. I guess he's right. Sometimes, karma is a snickerdoodle.

Tony, age 15-1/2